OWL

LIFE CYCLES

Words that look like **this** can be found in the glossary on page 24.

NOTTINGHAMSHIRE EDUCATION LIBRARY SERVICE	
E220208905	
Askews & Holts	17-Feb-2021
598.97	

BookLife
PUBLISHING

©2018
BookLife Publishing
King's Lynn
Norfolk PE30 4LS

All rights reserved.
Printed in Malaysia.

A catalogue record for this book is available from the British Library.

ISBN: 978-1-78637-378-6

Written by:
Madeline Tyler

Edited by:
Kirsty Holmes

Designed by:
Danielle Rippengill

All facts, statistics, web addresses and URLs in this book were verified as valid and accurate at time of writing. No responsibility for any changes to external websites or references can be accepted by either the author or publisher.

CONTENTS

Page 4	What Is a Life Cycle?
Page 5	What Is an Owl?
Page 6	Eggs
Page 8	Incubation
Page 10	Owlets
Page 12	Fledglings
Page 14	Owls
Page 16	Types of Owls
Page 18	Owl Facts
Page 20	World Record Breakers
Page 22	Life Cycle of an Owl
Page 23	Get Exploring!
Page 24	Glossary and Index

WHAT IS A LIFE CYCLE?

All animals, plants and humans go through different stages of their life as they grow and change. This is called a life cycle.

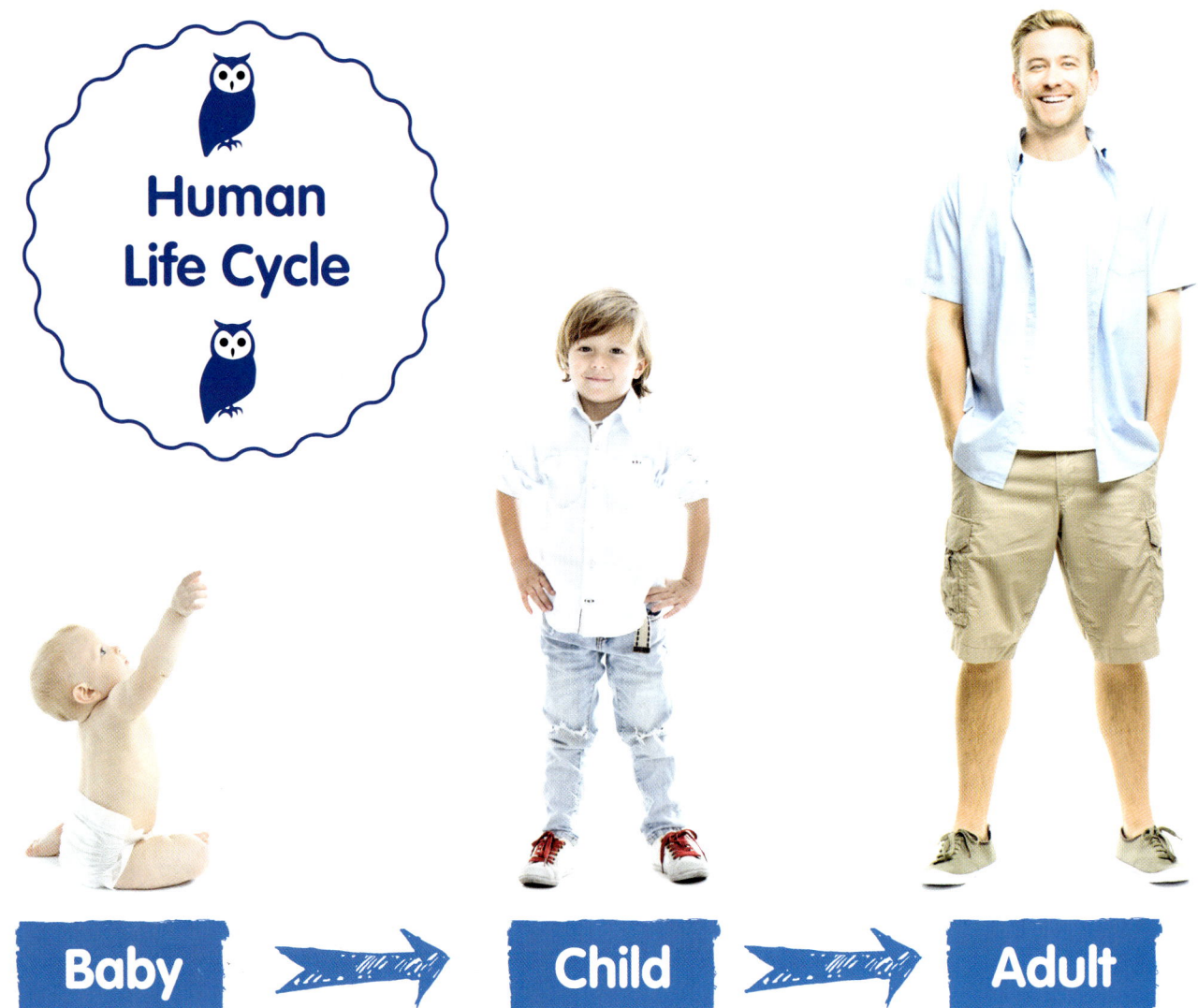

Baby → Child → Adult

WHAT IS AN OWL?

An owl is a type of bird. Owls have feathers, wings, long claws and sharp beaks. Owls have very good hearing and eyesight, which makes them good hunters.

EGGS

Female owls lay their eggs in nests. Many owls use nests that have been built and **abandoned** by other birds.

Nests are usually high up in trees.

Owls lay between five and eight eggs in their nests. One egg is laid every three days. The group of eggs is called a clutch.

INCUBATION

After she has laid her eggs, the female owl sits on them to keep them warm. This is called incubation.

Incubation lasts for around 35 days. After this, the eggs begin to hatch in the same order that they were laid.

OWLETS

Young owls are called owlets. They use a special egg tooth to break the egg. When they first hatch, owlets are covered in tiny, fluffy feathers called down.

Owlet

Owls eat insects, fish, and small mammals like mice.

Owlets cannot fly or find their own food. The father owl brings food back to the nest and the mother owl breaks it up for the owlets.

FLEDGLINGS

When the owlets are about one month old, they begin to grow adult feathers. As they grow bigger, the owlets become fledglings.

Fledglings still have some down.

The fledglings can now practice flying with their new feathers Fledglings cannot fly very far because their wings are not fully grown.

OWLS

The fledglings become adults when they are fully grown and have all their feathers. They can now fly and hunt for their own food.

The owls leave their parents' nest to find a **mate** and a nest of their own. Soon, the female owl will be ready to lay her own eggs.

Most owls only ever have one mate.

TYPES OF OWLS

There are over 200 different **species** of owl. Barn owls are very common all over the world and are found on almost every **continent**.

Barn Owl

Snowy Owl

Snowy owls live in very cold areas where there is a lot of snow. Their white feathers are a good **camouflage** because they are the same colour as snow.

OWL FACTS

Most owls are nocturnal. This means that they sleep during the daytime and come out at night to hunt for **prey**.

Owl Pellet

Owls often swallow their food whole. They cough up the bones and fur of their prey and spit it out as an owl pellet.

WORLD RECORD BREAKERS

World's Farthest Head-Spin

Owls can **rotate** their heads the farthest of any animal — 270 degrees! This is almost all the way round!

Largest Collection of Owls

A man called Yaakov Chai set the world record for the largest collection of objects that look like owls. In 2016, the collection was made up of 19,100 owl objects.

LIFE CYCLE OF AN OWL

1 A female owl lays her eggs in another bird's abandoned nest.

2 The owl incubates her eggs until they hatch. They come out covered in down.

LIFE CYCLES

4 The adult owls leave their parents to find a mate and a new nest.

3 The owlets grow feathers and become fledglings.

Get Exploring!

Have you ever seen an owl in your local area? Visit a zoo or a bird **sanctuary** to learn more about different types of owls.

GLOSSARY

abandoned left behind to never be returned to

camouflage traits that allow an animal to hide itself in a habitat

continent a very large area of land that is made up of many countries

mammals animals that have warm blood, a backbone and produce milk

mate a partner (of the same species) who an animal chooses to produce young with

prey animals that are hunted by other animals for food

rotate turn around a central point

sanctuary a nature reserve; somewhere that offers protection to wildlife

species a group of very similar animals or plants that are capable of producing young together

INDEX

barn owls 16

down 10, 12, 22

eggs 6–10, 15, 22

feathers 5, 10, 12–14, 17, 22

fledglings 12–14, 22

incubation 8–9, 22

mate 15, 22

nests 6–7, 11, 15, 22

owl pellet 19

owlets 10–12, 22

snowy owls 17

wings 5, 13

zoo 23

PHOTO CREDITS

All images are courtesy of Shutterstock.com, unless otherwise specified. With thanks to Getty Images, Thinkstock Photo and iStockphoto. Frontcover – Rosa Jay. 1 – Rosa Jay. 2 – duangnapa_b. 3 – Maksimilian, Toukung design, Rosa Jay.. 4 – Africa Studio, ESB Professional, Aila Images. 5 – Anan Kaewkhammul. 6 – Mark Caunt. 7 – Vishnevskiy Vasily. 8 – PetraMenclovaCZ. 9 – Pictureguy. 10 – Kurit afshen. 11 – Mriya Wildlife. 12 – Gina Hendrick. 13 – Captivelight. 14 – Mriya Wildlife. 15 – Toppy Berry. 16 – duangnapa_b. 17 – Jim Cumming. 18 – BMJ. 19 – picturepartners. 20 & 21 – Maquiladora. 22 – Maksimilian, Florian Teodor, BIOphotos, Mr. JIRAKRIT SITTIWONG. 23 – ChameleonsEye.